REAL ESTATE
TREASURE MAP

Your Personal Guide to Real Estate Riches

By Tim & Julie Harris

Edited by A. B. Guitry

TABLE OF CONTENTS

Introduction to your new Business Plan – Your Treasure Map for Success

Now that you have your Treasure Map, it's important to recognize that you are on a journey this year – that you must start with the end in mind. It will take all 365 days for you to achieve all of your goals and dreams. You have taken the first step by deciding to create your map and follow it. Understanding the **Five Stages of Mastery** is critical to enhancing your chances of staying on course.

What you are about to learn is based on tens of thousands of coaching calls with fellow real estate agents and years of personal experience selling hundreds of homes. Chances are, what you are about to read may in some cases confront your beliefs about yourself and your real estate business. If you do feel some discomfort as you read this book I want to congratulate you.

Why?

Simple, it's because you are willing to be uncomfortable. You are the rare person who is willing to accept that change is not only okay but also absolutely necessary. You see, nothing stays the same. It's against the laws of nature for anything to stay the same. You already know this. You know that you must change daily, especially in THIS real estate market. Everything that you took for granted about the real estate industry has changed. And we are just getting started.

Over the next few years we will see massive changes to the way nearly every aspect of the real estate business is conducted. Let me say that again, as it's crucial that you understand and accept this point. Everything in the real estate industry, from the way you generate your business, earn your commission, secure a mortgage – everything is changing. Do not think for a moment that what you know today is sufficient for what will be required in the market as it evolves over the next 24 to 36 months. Not a day goes by that we don't hear a fellow real estate educator telling agents to "Get back to the basics." It makes sense, but what does an agent do when the "basics" themselves are changing?

The largest changes in any industry always happen during a recession or a time of economic crisis. What our industry is experiencing now is the complete turning inside out of everything we have taken for granted. Don't have fear; don't for a moment think that you don't have what it takes to thrive during and after these changes. But, you must always be learning. As a matter of fact, you must be on the absolute ragged edge of what is next for the real estate industry. Again, change is inevitable; whether you will or you will not remain in the real estate business is not inevitable. It's up to you to adapt and to look for what's next, to always be learning.

In a recent interview with Gregg Neuman, who has been the number one Prudential agent in the world for four of the last eight years, we discussed this very topic. Gregg made the comment that:

There are three things every agent must be focused on at all times:

1. Going on Appointments
2. Generating Leads
3. Learning

Allow the change. Welcome the change. Look for ways to change.

Agents spend a lot of time making plans: 30-day plans, 90-day plans, business plans, action plans, plans to get out of debt, savings plans, weight-loss plans. Agents make these plans with all of the right intentions. They want to have a plan that will allow for change. It makes perfect sense that you might want to have a specific, detailed plan to evoke change. But regardless of how many plans you make or how well-intended they were, why is it that so few of us ever actually experience any real meaningful change?

The old-fashioned way of thinking will tell you that you simply didn't want the "change" badly enough or you didn't make enough effort. Strictly speaking, if more effort and "work" were the magic formula, then the hardest working among us would be getting the best results and having the most success. We know that's not true. Simply working harder doesn't guarantee you anything.

Why?

Because you may be using the wrong tools. You may be using old techniques, old scripts, old methods that simply won't work in this market.

Dr. Lair Ribeiro, in his wonderful book, *Success Is No Accident,* makes a statement that is powerful in its simplicity. "If you go on doing what you've always done, you'll go on getting what you've always got." If you are truly ready to make changes in your business, you have to change the ways in which you are doing things. Let's be clear about something: your skills and what you know worked great for you in the previous hot seller's market. You had to learn how to sell in that market. If you think back, you will remember that learning those skills required that you change from whatever way you were thinking previously. Many of you have only sold real estate in a hot seller's market. If this is true for you, your path to change may be more of a struggle than it should be.

At HREU, we have had literally tens of thousands of coaching calls with agents. Many of those agents were simply unwilling to change, even when their efforts clearly were not working. They actually believed that what worked in the past, super hot, almost *insane* seller's market would work in this market. Nothing could be further from the truth. Agents are often very fearful of change. It's common for agents to say things like:

"I've always done things this way."

"I'm just not that kind of person."

"There is only one way to do things and that's the way I am doing them!"

These agents are stuck in the past. If you want to not only survive but also thrive in this market you must remember that if you keep doing what you have always done, you will go on getting what you have always got. If what you were doing simply doesn't work in this market and you continue to do it, then your only other option will be to leave the real estate business.

There are countless examples of where an unwillingness to try something new, or an unwillingness to do something differently, will interfere with your chances of success. Make a list of everything in your business that is being done in exactly the same way it was being done 12 to 24 months ago. Remember, this new market requires that you change.

Ask yourself these questions:

1. **Have I changed the way I generate leads?**
2. **Have I changed the way I do listing presentations?**
3. **Have I changed my prelisting package to reflect this market? (Do you even have a prelisting package?)**

4. **Do you use memorized scripts and presentations that reflect this market?**
5. **Have I upgraded my skills, or learned skills to work with buyers?**
6. **Do I consider myself the best buyer's agent?**
7. **Do I consider myself the best listing agent?**

Let's talk a little more about change. John Fisher created a great explanation to describe the process of change. This is the process that all of us go through when we are experiencing change. Now that you know that change is required for this market, look at the next page and ask yourself where you are in this process.

The Stages of Change

Anxiety

"Can I deal with this change? Am I ready? Do I know enough? What will happen if I don't change?" Caution: Don't allow yourself to go into denial. Anxiety will go away as you progress to the next stage.

Happiness

"Hurrah! Something is going to change. I am excited that I can feel things are finally moving forward. I can now feel like I am actually headed in the right direction. I want to tell the world!"

Fear

"Oh boy, here it comes. Can I really deal with this change? What will my family and friends think? What will the other agents think? Can I handle the success or potential failure?" Caution: At this stage of change, the ego often comes into play. Deepak Chopra said that, "All fear is based in ego. The ego creates fear to stop the change."

Threat

"Let's get ready to rumble. What will the other agent do when I change? What will happen? Who will attack me? Will I get sued?" Caution: Watch out that you don't allow yourself to start to experience disillusionment or a feeling of no longer caring.

Guilt

"I can't BELIEVE that I actually believed that before. I can't believe that I spend SO much time doing something so ridiculous." Caution: Don't allow yourself to become depressed at this stage. You need to forgive yourself and move on.

Gradual Acceptance
"Okay, I am here – that is the past – I am moving forward."

Moving Forward
"Wow! This is really going to work!"

Where are you in this process? Have you been stuck at one of these levels of change and don't know what to do next? You are not alone.

Take a moment to take a very deep breath and know that you are not alone. This real estate market has been one of the *most challenging* real estate markets ever. Many industry experts are calling this the worst real estate market in the history of the United States! No wonder change can be difficult, especially when everything is changing!

Here is what you do now.

Accept where you are in the process and make a commitment to move forward. You can do it. Think of it this way: what options do you really have?

Now it's up to you. Only you. You don't have to go it alone anymore.

The Five Levels of Required Learning to Become a Superstar

Level 1
Clueless Know Nothings

When you don't know what you don't know!

You can easily identify an agent at this first phase, Clueless Know Nothing, because they typically have few or no real skills, they don't keep any sort of schedule, and have no clue where their next lead is going to come from, let alone their next paycheck. 95% of all agents are at this stage. You are probably at this stage.

We call this stage Clueless Know Nothings because these agents have no clue that they don't have a clue.

Are you at this level?

Take this simple test. Be honest with yourself and don't cheat and try to "skip a step." Then read the results key.

1. Do you have a set schedule designed around predetermined goals? **Yes/No**

2. Do you frequently attend any and all "educational events" offered by your office, your region, and your MLS board because you think this is the best use of your time? **Yes/No**

3. Do you track all of your numbers? (No, not your phone numbers.) Do you know your cost per lead, cost per transaction, profit per sale, etc.? **Yes/No**

4. Do you have an organized database of past clients and centers of influence that you hear from at least once per month? **Yes/No**

5. Do you have a belief that the agents who are successful have a secret or are in some way cheating to obtain their success? **Yes/No**

If you answered No to more than three of these questions, you are at this level. Remember, 95% of agents are at this level. You are not alone.

Characteristics of an agent at this level:

1. They think they know it all. In other words, they actually believe that they have it all "sorted out."
2. They badmouth or go out of their way to deny the importance of learning anything new.
3. Most importantly, they have no clue that they know nothing. (Thus, the name, Clueless Know Nothings.)

Clueless Know Nothings are easy to spot. When Julie and I speak at our events, the Clueless Know Nothings always sit in the back of the room with their arms crossed. They are the ones who show up late and leave early. Worse yet, at break times they are the ones who will try to convince you that you don't need to change.

Are you feeling a bit uncomfortable because you now realize that you too are at this first level? Do you perhaps feel a little queasy? Maybe you feel a little nervous.

Perfect.

Why?

Because in order to grow to the next level, you MUST be okay with being uncomfortable. Most people spend their entire lives doing everything in their power to avoid ever feeling uncomfortable. They build their lives around never feeling uncomfortable. Maybe now, for the first time in a very long time you are feeling a little uncomfortable. Allow yourself to feel this way. It's necessary.

Our goal is to move you to the next level as quickly as you will allow. Let me repeat: as quickly as YOU will allow. You will allow this to happen only when you realize that you are clueless. You must allow yourself the opportunity to move forward and this will only happen when you consciously accept the fact that you are clueless. Be okay with being clueless. Accept it! Heck, it's better than where you were back when you were at Level 1 as a Clueless Know Nothing!

You are now on your way. That feeling that you have, the feeling of anxiety, the feeling of being a little scared and nervous, of being uncomfortable, don't fight it. Be okay with feeling that way. It's a sign that you are changing. Congratulations!

As you progress from level to level you will sense a feeling of awakening. You will have an "a-ha" moment. Look for those feelings. As your coach I don't really think that I am teaching you anything new. The simple fact is that you already have the seeds of greatness within you. You already possess everything that you need to live the life of your dreams. It's my job and the job of everyone at HREU to ignite the spark inside you that creates the flame of change. Feel the knowingness that only comes when you are on the right path.

KNOW that you are now on the right path.

Level 2
Knowing Know Nothings

Welcome to Level 2. This is where your life gets interesting. Once you have accepted the fact that you are clueless, you will start to truly learn and grow. You have transcended from being a "knows not" to a "knowing knows not." That may not sound good, but believe me, you are doing well. Remember, 95% of all agents never progress beyond Level 1. Don't celebrate just yet. Put those bottles of Cristal back into the cooler. Before we move on let me warn you about something:

You can easily regress back to the first level. Indeed it's very common for agents to regress back to the first level. Why? Because at Level 2 and beyond, you have to practice and exercise your soon to be newly-learned skills. It's all too easy and very common for the "wing it" approach to creep back in. Agents learn a thing or two, figure out a few things, and then all of a sudden they are back to where they started. They "know it all," when in reality they are back to being Clueless Know Nothings. Make a commitment that you won't allow this to happen to you.

Here is the test to determine if you are a Level 2 Knowing Know-Nothing:

Ask yourself these five questions. Be 100% honest.

1. Do you know that there are many things that you don't know? **Yes/No**

2. Have you attended a professional educational event where you walked out and thought, "I know more than that clown. I should be a speaker!" **Yes/No**

3. Have you attempted to adapt something new to your business or maybe recently read a book or exposed yourself to someone or something that you never have before in your life? **Yes/No**

4. Do you know that you can no longer simply wing it?
Yes/No

5. Are you finally willing to admit that you don't really
know it all? **Yes/No**

**If you answered Yes to three or more of these questions, you
are at Level 2.**

Let me tell you from a coach's perspective, I love agents who
are at this level. Why? They are ready to learn. They have
accepted that they need help and far more importantly, they are
ready to take action. Level 1 agents are nearly impossible to
coach. They actually believe that they have it all figured out. If
you are a Level 2 agent, know that you are at a critical time.

**If you want to continue on your upward path, follow these
suggestions:**

1. **Build your business around a proven model.** The
"a little of this and a little of that" approach won't
work. Whatever models you follow make sure it's
NOT dependent on only one source of generating
leads. You must have a balanced approach to your
business. At HREU we coach students to have four
or five unique and separate sources for their lead
generation. That way if one goes away you are still
okay because the others will pick up the slack. We
call this "Building Your Wheel."

2. **Be uncomfortable; avoid being "comfortable."**
Give yourself permission to be uncomfortable – as
much as possible.

3. **Accept the fact that you must practice, you must
train**. Becoming competent, let alone mastering
anything, requires constant practice. Thomas Edison
said that you couldn't consider yourself an expert at

anything until you have done the same thing 10,000 times. Here is a secret: never allow yourself to think that you have mastered anything. Julie and I have gone on hundreds if not thousands of listing appointments and I can tell you, we still have a lot to learn. We have had tens of thousands of personal, one-on-one coaching calls with agents just like you, and not a day goes by that we don't continue to learn. Always be learning – never let yourself feel like you have learned it all, heard it all before, or know it all.

4. **Avoid the Helpful Opinions and Free Advice of others**. Most people don't consciously intend to be harmful with their free advice. Accept the fact that when you are growing and changing you WILL make others uncomfortable. You are forcing others to look inward and ask the difficult questions that they may have been avoiding their entire lives. You see, they are almost certainly at the first level, wanting you to be back there with them. However, sometimes this "helpful advice" comes from people who are in positions of leadership.

5. **Ego**. Ego gives us the inner strength that we all need to grow and move forward. Ego is a powerful ally but can also be our worst enemy. Here is a clue that your ego may be in your way: Fear. Fear is Ego; Ego is Fear. When you feel fear of any kind it's because the ego is in defense mode. Let me be clear about something. Fear has its role. If you are about to be eaten by a shark, fear is nature's response to danger. But chances are you are not going to be on any predator's menu anytime soon, so fear not! Your ego doesn't want you to change. Fears such as "maybe I can't handle the success," or more commonly, "maybe I can't handle the failure" — all of those feelings are ego-based.

At this stage you must get into action. Massive inspired action. Now is when you hire a coach. Follow in the path of others. Don't waste time or energy trying to do it "your way." Don't create. DO copy. Use the scripts, the presentations, and the systems that have already been tested and proven to work.

The absolute worst thing for you to do when you are at this stage is overwhelm yourself with too many competing messages. Focus is the key.

Okay, I am going to warn you now that what I am about to tell you will sound a little self-serving. I am going to talk about how to hire a coach. As you know, Harris Real Estate University is in the business of coaching real estate agents. So with that in mind, use these questions when interviewing a potential coach. Listen, you will be spending money on coaching. At this stage in your development, hiring a coach is the smartest thing to do. A great coach will save you time, hold you accountable, and call you out when you are being a goofball.

Warning: What you are about to read may cause you discomfort. Ouch, there is that word again!

The Top Five Questions You Must Ask When Interviewing a Coach:

1. How long have you been selling or did you ever sell real estate?

You may find this hard to believe, but people who have never sold real estate are running many of the coaching businesses in our industry, or they haven't sold real estate since the Great Depression. Remember those great Holiday Inn Express commercials where the guy runs into the operating room dressed as a surgeon and the nurse asks if he has ever performed this operation before and the guy responds, "No, but I stayed at a Holiday Inn Express last night"? Would you want that guy operating on you? The bottom line is that these coaching companies are NOT in the real estate business. They are not like you and me! They are in the "selling stuff to real estate agents" business. They are professional "Selling Stuff to Agents" sales people. Everyone who works at HREU sells real estate, and is highly successful doing so.

2. What is your coaching program's suggested form of lead generation?

This question will get me into trouble for suggesting that you ask it. Why? Because most coaches and coaching companies take an "it's my way or the highway" approach to lead generation. If you do your research, you will discover that there is the "prospecting over the phone" coaching company, the "branding and look at me marketing" coaching company, the "mail stuff to your centers of influence all the time in hopes that they will use you" coaching company, and the "run crafty ads trying get them to call you" coaching company. Not to mention all the hundreds of companies that are in the business of selling leads to agents via their websites and may also offer coaching. Let me be clear, all of these approaches have their merits. Where they fall short is that they will tell you that it's their way or the highway. Does that really work for you? Do you do well when you are given no options? Of course not. HREU's approach is balanced; you will have four or five well-defined sources for your leads. We call this the "spokes to your wheel." The more spokes, and the stronger the spokes, the better the wheel. These other coaching companies would have you believe that you can do just one thing and build your business. That's nuts. We know and/or have coached some of the most successful agents in the US. None of them do just one thing to generate their leads.

3. Who will coach me?

Watch out for this one. Its not uncommon that we hear horror stories from agents who have been with other coaching companies who had coaches who were LESS experienced in real estate than they were! I will tell you this and you will think that I am putting you on: there are coaching companies who have coaches who have never sold real estate. They are basically telemarketers reading a script. You must know who will be your coach. Have they coached before? Who have they coached before and what were the results? All HREU coaches are seasoned agents. They have sold and are selling in this market. In addition to that, Julie and myself personally coach them.

4. Is my coaching experience a one size fits all approach, or is it designed around my strengths and my needed areas of improvement?

This is a fun one. Remember when I told you that most coaching companies have coaches that simply read scripts and follow the same road map for every client? You sign up for coaching expecting a highly personalized, professional relationship. What you often get is quite the opposite. At HREU there are no pre-written coaching calls, no one size fits all coaching programs. Your experience with your coach at HREU is designed around you, pure and simple.

5. Are your coaching programs and teachings based on today's way of selling homes, or techniques that are now outdated and no longer relevant?

Think about that for a moment. You would be amazed to learn that there are coaching companies who base all of their teachings on approaches that came about decades ago. Sure, in some cases the old school way of doing things still works. But if you are going to be in business in THIS real estate market you have to embrace change. (There is that word again – keeps cropping up, doesn't it?)
You have hired a coach; you have accepted change. You are learning.

Now it is time to introduce you to the next level of learning.

Welcome to: **Knowing Can-Do**.

Level 3
Knowing Can-Dos

You may never have experienced this level at anytime in your life before. I don't say that lightly. It takes a special person to achieve this level.

<u>Tim's Story</u>

I was a lot like many of you probably are. I had enough natural sales skills that I could sell anything. I had existed until my mid-twenties off my natural abilities and refused to learn. I would have been the world's worst coaching client. It's easy for me to recognize what stage a coaching client is in because I was like many of you. I lived for years at Level 1. What changed me?

I reached my natural limits. Our real estate business sold 100 homes consistently, but we wanted to sell more. Julie knew that we had to learn from others but I was a complete butthead and didn't listen. Heck, we didn't need no stinking coach! After all, we sold 100 homes our first year in the business. I actually believed that "I knew it all."

Julie knew differently. She is a classically-trained musician. She has always had coaches and private mentors.

One day we were listening to an interview with a top agent in the nation. What we learned from him shocked us. He was not only selling 300+ homes per year, he had done that after only three years in the business. Well, that's all it took. We, or rather I, finally awakened to the path that I am sharing with you now.

That's when Julie and I hired our first coach. Although technically, coaching as it is today wasn't really around, so we paid this person $5,000 to spend the day with him. I remember that day clearly all these years later. We learned what it took to go to the next level. We had acquired the tools and were learning the skills to grow our business.

Are you at this level now? Are you a Knowing Can-Do? Ask yourself these questions. Again, no looking forward to the answers.

1. Are you using prepared or maybe "canned" scripts and presentations? **Yes/No**

2. Are you practicing the skills necessary to learn and continue to grow? **Yes/No**

3. Are you starting to see consistent cash flow, taking and selling listings on a regular basis? **Yes/No**

4. Are you constantly aware of the fact that you have a long way to go and you are thrilled about the challenge as opposed to scared of the changes necessary? **Yes/No**

5. Are you setting aside Fear and Doubt and replacing those feelings with Action and Effort? **Yes/No**

If you answered YES to more than three of these questions, you are a Knowing Can-Do.

But Watch Out!

This is the level that requires the most effort. Not just a little extra effort here and there but massive consistent action every day. When you are a Knowing Can-Do, you must practice every day, all the time. You have to live and breathe your scripts, and your presentations. You have to work daily from a schedule and accept outside accountability. If you don't work intensely, if you don't accept accountability and stay focused, your tenure as a Knowing Can-Do will be very short-lived. And if you fall from this level you will probably fall back to being a Clueless Know Nothing. Please don't let that happen to you. At this stage you MUST have a coach. **Must**, not maybe. Warning: Fighting this simple fact means that you already have one foot out the door and are sliding back to being a Clueless Know Nothing.

Characteristics of a Knowing Can-Do

1. You now have a "canned, pre-prepared" approach to virtually all aspects of your business. You can perform your listing presentation at the highest of level at the drop of a hat.

2. You know what you are doing and how to do it, but you still have to think about what you are doing. You take written scripts with you to listing presentations. You follow a script when you do virtually everything.

3. You don't need constant handholding or feedback. You are confident in your skills and know that when you follow your presentation and your plan you will succeed.

4. Fear no longer rules your life. You no longer are governed by your fears. What others say or think about you has become less and less important.

5. Your office is probably starting to recognize you for taking listings, having sales, etc. Maybe they are asking if you would like to teach something at the next office meeting. WARNING: Don't do it. Avoid the adulation of others. Be polite and gently decline the offers. Your goal is to ascend to the highest levels, not to become the office presenter.

The most important word that summarizes this stage is Practice. You must practice constantly.

Take suggestions for practicing and reinforcement of your learning. Your coach will help you with additional approaches.

1. Make an audio recording of your next listing presentation and have your coach critique it for you. Set your ego aside. Be open and welcoming to the opportunity to learn and grow from feedback from your coach.

2. Use scripts that have been proven to work in this market. Handwrite or copy the scripts ten times a day until you know them cold. We have had many coaching clients tell us that doing this was the single most significant way for them to learn. Scripts you must know cold are: Centers of Influence/Past Clients, For Sale By Owners, Expireds, Listing Presentation, Pre-Qualifying, Lead Follow-Up, IVR/1800homehotline.com call back script, etc. If I called you in the middle of the night and asked for you to recite to me the Lead Follow-Up script you would have to be able do it instantly. When I say learn the scripts cold, I mean it.

Role-play your scripts with others. Every morning at the same time, set time aside to have an actual live role-play with other agents who are at the same level as you.

There are many other great ways to practice that you will learn from your coach.

It bears repeating that it's very easy to fall from this level. What often happens is that agents refuse to maintain the commitment of time and energy to practicing and staying coachable. As I write this I can think of many coaching clients who worked their butts off to get to this level but simply refused to make the consistent effort to stay there.

Of course, agents slide down for other reasons as well.

One of the biggest reasons is that they don't surround themselves with other like-minded agents. There is an old example that I always give on coaching calls to explain this to agents:

Imagine a large bucket with a single crab in it. That crab will get out of that bucket almost instantly. He has no problem chucking his large claw over the edge and boom, he is out of that bucket and off he goes.

Now, put two or more crabs in that same bucket and they will stay in the bucket. One crab will try to get out and the other will pull him back down. I have actually seen this happen. No matter what, when there are two or more crabs in a bucket there will be no escapees. They will do whatever it takes to hold each other back, even if it means their certain doom.

Often, agents' behavior is like the crabs in the bucket. When one is trying to escape, the others will pull him or her back down.

DON'T LET THAT HAPPEN TO YOU.

You have to go out of your way to avoid anyone and everyone who is not on the same path you are on. Avoid the agents who are not on the same level or higher than you. Here is the hard part:

That means that you will need to accept the fact that many of the people you thought were your friends were not. They were simply other crabs sharing the same bucket as you. Remember, I said that staying at this level would require effort. I didn't hold anything back when I told you that it's very common for agents to slide back from this level.

Five Things You Must Do to Avoid Reversal of Fortune and Sliding Back From This Level

1. Stay connected with other like-minded people. If you don't know anyone in your office or maybe even your community, look to your coach to help you form a Master Mind group.

2. This is a difficult one – avoid 99% of the traditional real estate agent events. If your office has a Must Attend Policy for their weekly meetings, then go. But avoid the water cooler talk.

3. Do exactly what your coach tells you. All of the HREU coaches know this process and have passed through these levels. They know what you are feeling and experiencing.

4. Exposure. Go out of your way to expose yourself to new people, places, and ideas. Start small by going to different restaurants or maybe decide that you will take a vacation to a part of the world that you have never been.

5. Have two to three big, meaty goals. Find two or three things that really excite you: travel, a new car, shopping for a brand new wardrobe. Here is an interesting fact: anyone who has ever accomplished anything of note knows the importance of always being "current." They always have new clothes and are open to the latest trends. It's also a great idea to have smaller goals to keep you on track. Julie recently rewarded herself with a new iPhone because she had accomplished a personal goal that she had set for herself.

Are you ready for the next level? If so, let's move on.

Level 4
The Autopilot

At this stage in your development you have come to a place few will ever reach. The air is certainly rarified at this level. You have accomplished something that will allow you to transcend the very things that once required high levels of effort. You have internalized on a subconscious level most of what is necessary for you to continue on your path to the highest peaks. Everything comes naturally. You don't have to think about what you will say or do. Whatever you say or do is almost always perfect. There isn't a situation that you can't handle effortlessly. People think you are a "natural." Everything seems to happen for you almost magically.

Are you the Autopilot?
Ask yourself these questions.

1. Can you enter into any situation with any seller, buyer, or agent, no matter how challenging, and naturally, without any forethought, know just what to say and do? **Yes/No**

2. Does your work feel like it does when you are driving your car? In other words, you don't have to consciously think about what to do, you simply *know*. **Yes/No**

3. You can negotiate a contract, delegate to your staff while you are returning an email, and have everything work perfectly? **Yes/No**

4. Do you have an almost natural ability to teach others, but it's challenging for you to explain what to do? Is this because you no longer have to actually think since everything for you happens on autopilot? **Yes/No**

Free Coaching Call? http://1on1coaching.com

5. Do you perhaps find yourself a little bored and feeling a lack of challenge? **Yes/No**

If you answered Yes to more than three of these questions, you are at Level 4. You are the Autopilot. At this stage you have the opportunity to achieve truly great things. The constant practicing of the previous stages has paid off, and now everything in your business seems to happen with virtually no effort.

Challenges at this level:

1. **Complacency**. You are someone who has gone far beyond the norm for most people. You now posses a level of deep unconscious knowing that gives you a sense of freedom and security that nothing else ever will. You have to continue to learn and challenge yourself. If you allow yourself to become complacent you will be like the superstar Formula One racecar driver who never lost a race, but is now constantly driving into walls. When a person continues to practice the skill that has become second nature, but over time allows negative habits to form, they will slide back. Complacency also happens when a person becomes tied to one way of doing something and is no longer open to new, up-to-date skills. Nothing stays the same. Change is constant, even when you are the Autopilot.

A longtime friend and HREU Superstar, Linda McKissick, experienced what can happen at this level. She and her husband Jim had built a real estate business that consistently sold over 300 homes per year. One day she woke up and asked herself, "Is this it, am I at the top? Is selling 300 homes per year all I am or can do?" She had built her business to the point where it was on autopilot and she was on autopilot as well. She realized that she had become complacent. That day she decided to recommit to learning. She decided that she wanted to go to her next level. Eight years later she had created several other businesses and now makes nearly $2 million per year, passively. You see, Linda knew the path; she knew the power of learning and the levels that she had to pass through. To hear Linda's Free Superstar interview go to: www.harrisrealestateuniversity.com.

2. **Recreating Yourself.** When you are at this level you now possess a level of knowledge about real estate that is so internal, you don't actually have to think. Your actions, your words, your results happen almost without effort. Now it's time for you to decide what is next. Will it be a new business or maybe you will go back to school? You don't have fears that you can't continue to be successful. You don't have fears of lack. You now must find something that allows you to transcend to the next level.

To do this you will need to find others who are also at Level 4, you will need them in order to transcend to Level 5.

Level 5
Enlightened Mastery

At this level the agent has not only mastered the physical skill of real estate at the highest level but has transcended to the next level. At this level, the agent does not require conscious, deliberate, and careful execution of the skill but instead operates instinctively and reflexively. A minimum effort is required with maximum output resulting is their norm. At this level he is able to understand the very dynamics of his own physical skills. He understands, comprehends fully and accurately the what, when, how, and why of his own skill. Enlightened Mastery means that you react intuitively to any new situation with optimal results. He is constantly introspective, aware of his thoughts, and choosing his actions. His results are no longer tied to the ebb and flow of emotions.

Enlightened Mastery means that the agent now fully understands all of the necessary components of the skill to be learned. At this level, the actual physical energy required to accomplish tasks is minimal. People at this level are always the best teachers, coaches, and leaders.

You can recognize people at this level because they always seem to be "in the zone," "in the flow," or "wired in." When you are at Level 5 your actions are no longer governed by slow deliberate thoughts. People at this level don't use words that indicate any lack. There are no limitations and no boundaries for Level 5 Agents.

Level 5 Agents are fully aware of their level of consciousness. You can operate with fluency and effortlessness from an instinctive level. You are able to articulate what you are doing for yourself and others. At this level, other people are naturally attracted to you. People often seek your advice and coaching.

None of us has any choice but to accept change. You now have the power to create positive change or allow the effects of our indecision and inaction to dictate the change for you. Our bodies are constantly changing. Scientists tell us that by the time we are forty-five years old, our bodies have regenerated our entire skeletal system. Every year 98% of the atoms in your body are regenerated.

I will give you two examples:

Agent A

Agent A, let's call her Mary, has been in the real estate business for five years. Her entire career has been in a dramatically increasing seller's market. The norm in her area for home appreciation is less than 6% per year, but over the last three years alone, homes have gone up over 30%. Mary has been able to have sizable increases in her income year after year. Her office has often rewarded her for her success. Mary didn't need to know much in terms of sales skills, presentation skills, objection handlers, etc. In her market, homes practically sold themselves. Buyers flocked to buy every listing because they wanted to cash in on the super hot seller's market. Owning a home in Mary's market was akin to buying the winning lottery ticket. Mary was the classic "wing it" type and because of the nature of the market she was doing just fine.

Then, almost overnight it seemed, the market completely changed.

Mary's homes no longer sold themselves. She never developed buyer skills so she had no clue how to work buyers. It had become common for homeowners to actually owe more on their homes than the market would pay. Mary, who was seeing dramatic increases in her income year after year, was now finding herself almost broke. She, like so many others, was avoiding change.

But Mary did something about it.

She accepted the fact that she was a Clueless Know Nothing and decided to learn. She decided to invest in herself and her future. It wasn't easy for her. Remember, for Mary, it all seemed so easy – before. She accepted the fact that she needed to change, and as a result she is now learning the skills necessary to get back on track and regain her success. She accepted change; she accepted the fact that she needed to learn.

Agent B

Unfortunately Agent B, let's call him Mike, is far more common than Mary. Mike, like Mary, had only sold real estate in a super hot, rapidly appreciating seller's market. Mike had not only been rewarded for his sales through steady increases in his income, but the local real estate board had awarded him with all kinds of plaques and trophies. Mike's office bookshelf was filled with these awards. If you were to see Mike's office and all the awards, you would think that he had won just about every real estate award available.

Mike's market changed.

He had built his success using techniques, scripts, and systems that worked wonderfully in the seller's market. Mike had it "down cold." But what he knew so well simply didn't work at the same level now. Mike had to change. But he couldn't, or at least he wouldn't allow himself to.

He thought that if he simply worked harder, worked longer hours, and took more and more listings, that everything would be okay. In theory his plan made sense. You absolutely have to put forth effort – massive effort – in this market. There are no shortcuts. However, the tools and techniques, the scripts and dialogues that were so ingrained in Mike's head, simply didn't seem to work. He didn't understand why what had worked so well before, now seemed not to work at all. He refused to change. Mike wouldn't accept the fact that the market had changed and that he had to change with the market.

Mike was slowly going broke. He had the listings but they weren't selling. He had the motivation but he didn't have the necessary new skills. He refused to change. Eventually, Mike will run out of savings, max out all of his credit cards, HELOC money, and will quietly leave the real estate industry.

Don't allow that to happen to you.

What you need to learn isn't any more difficult, more complicated, or requiring of more time and energy than what you were doing before. I am not asking you to stop doing what you are doing that is working. My intention is for you to accept the fact that change is not an option. Accept it.

The solution is to make the decision now, today, to TAKE ACTION, to follow all steps in the creation of your Treasure Map so that you will have a clear business plan this year. Follow it and it leads to riches. Skip steps and the map will be ineffective. The choice is yours. Either way, you know that we will be with you every step of the way here at Harris Real Estate University.

Goal Setting

I feel that the most important step in any major accomplishment is setting a specific goal. This enables you to keep your mind focused on your goal and off the many obstacles that will arise when you're striving to do your best.
Kurt Thomas

Without goals, your business plan won't have meaning. That's why we begin with what's important to you here at HREU and work from there.

Think of your business plan as a map. Let's say you were venturing out on a road trip. You're planning on driving from Burlington, VT, to San Francisco, CA, and along the way you plan to take in the sights. You pack up your gear and head south. You visit New York City first and then plan to get back on the road, pointing west to visit your cousins in Denver on the way out to San Francisco.

All of a sudden, you feel a sense of disorientation. You've never been in this state before, let alone on this road or at this intersection. You panic for a moment, but decide to follow your instinct and just go west.

A couple of hours later, you notice you're actually in Maryland. You're not going west at all. You should have taken a map. You should have listened to your friend that made this same trip last year and offered you a step-by-step guide. That wrong turn is going to add at least a day to your journey and you'll spend another $100 on gas unnecessarily. Unfortunately, that wasn't in your budget. You never make it to Denver and certainly not to San Francisco. Are you treating your goal setting the same way? You dream about all the things you want to do, see, and have, but you don't have a map to get you there.

What's a map?
Realistic, and Time
posted everywhere, of
going.

A map is something you refer
feel the panic you felt at that wro

You may be in uncharted waters rig
into one of several categories:

1. You're an experienced, top-producing
    high production and relatively easy and pre
    in the past. Your experience served you well u
    changed, and now you're having to change the
    business to get anywhere close to your previous pr

2. You're a brand new agent, and everything about real
    is uncharted territory.

3. You lie somewhere in between – you have some experience,
    you KNOW you can sell lots of homes, you're an expert in
    certain areas, but you also realize you're flying solo – you're
    not following any particular plan, you're just seeing what
    happens.

4. You're trying out real estate because it seems like something
    you could do. You may be from a different industry and real
    estate is now your only hope for an income this year. You
    have one foot in the real estate door and one foot out, you're
    "trying it out."

Agents in all of these categories need a MAP: a measurable,
specific PLAN for success. This map begins with deciding what
sights you want to see. What are the mile markers on the map?
What do you want to do, see, be, and have? What drives you?

GOAL SETTING is the first stage of mapping out your success.
So let's get started!

It's the Specific, Measurable, Attainable, ... (SMART) PLAN, written down and ... where you are now and where you're

...ost.

...to regularly, especially when you ...g turn, or in uncharted waters.

...t now. You probably fall

...gent who has had ...dictable business ...ntil the market ...way you do ...duction.

estate

...ived?

...ow will I do it?

- When will I do it by?

For example:
Most people say, "I want to get in better shape." But a specific goal would be, "On Monday, Wednesday, and Friday, I will attend a yoga class at Yogaworks, in Las Vegas, from noon to 1 p.m. On Tuesday and Thursday, I will hike for one hour at Red Rock Canyon."

Measurable

Establish concrete criteria for measuring progress toward the attainment of each goal you set. When you measure your progress, you stay on track, reach your target dates, and experience the sense of achievement that spurs you on to continued consistent effort that is necessary to achieve your specific goal.

To know if your goal is MEASURABLE, ask questions such as:

- How will I know if I'm in shape?
- How will I know I've made progress?
- What does it look like?
- How will I feel?

For example: I will know I am on track when I have been consistent with my workout schedule for at least 90 days. I will have a fitness expert track my heart rate and other measures of fitness and compare where I am when I begin working toward this goal, and how I'm doing each 90 days.

Attainable

After you have defined the goals that are most important to you, your next task is to figure out ways you can make the goals come true. You create the attitude, ability, skill, and financial capacity to reach them. You begin seeing opportunity everywhere that takes you closer and closer to attaining your goals.

Realistic

To be realistic, a goal must represent an objective toward which you are both *willing* and *able* to work. You are the only one who can decide just how high your goal should be. But be sure that every goal represents substantial progress. A lofty goal is frequently easier to reach than a low one because a low goal requires lower levels of energy and effort. Your goal is probably realistic if you truly *believe* that it can be accomplished. Additional ways to know if your goal is realistic is to determine if you have accomplished anything similar in the past. Or ask yourself what conditions would have to exist for you to accomplish this goal.

Timely
Your goals must have a specific, defined timeframe. If you lack a timetable, there will never be urgency – just as everyone says, "I want to get in better shape" each and every year. Those who write down their "get in shape" goal using the SMART rules are the ones who actually DO get in better shape. If you want to lose ten pounds, when do you want to lose it by? "Someday" won't work. But if you anchor it within a timeframe, let's say by June 1st for example, then you've set your unconscious mind into motion to begin working on the goal.

T can also stand for Tangible. A goal is tangible when you can experience it with one of the senses: taste, touch, smell, sight or hearing. When your goal is tangible, you have a better chance of making it specific, measurable, and attainable.

Our goals can only be reached through a vehicle of a plan, in which we must fervently believe, and upon which we must vigorously act. There is no other route to success.
Stephen A. Brennan

Proceed to: 'Understanding What it Takes to Achieve Your Goals.'

Understanding What It Takes to Achieve Your Goals

Use this brainstorming guide to discover what's really important to you and your family personally. This is where your powerful goal setting begins.

Take your time and think about your answers. No one is looking but you, so be honest and remember there are no right or wrong answers. Start by jotting down the first thing that comes to mind. This is not a ten-minute exercise. The time you spend now is critical to obtaining results.

In each category, jot down what you want, or think you want, your goals to be. Write your clearly defined, vivid, written objectives in all areas of your life. You can write and rewrite as you go. Make several copies of this exercise if you need to. This is a work in progress!

Use this worksheet to brainstorm. You'll *formalize* your *specific* goals using the format we've provided in a later section.

Each section has the same eleven questions to consider as you formulate what is important to you in each category. Answering these questions will help you define your goals and understand what it will likely take in order to ultimately achieve a positive outcome. Do not skip any of the eleven questions!

After brainstorming in this section, you'll be ready to move on to the **GOAL SETTING TEMPLATE,** where you'll *formalize your goals.* Do not skip ahead. You must complete this section first or your goals may be meaningless!

Secret: If you are still stuck, write down what you DON'T want in each category and build your goals around eliminating those fears.

Family Goals

Goal 1:

Goal 2:

Goal 3:

Where are you now vs. the desired outcome?

How will you feel when you have it?

How will you know when you have it?

What will this outcome accomplish for you?

Who else is involved or impacted by this goal?

Where, when, and how will you accomplish this?

What do you need to get your outcome?

Have you ever had or done this before? How did you do it?

Do you know anyone who has?

Can you act as if you have it?

Why do you want it?

Thoughts:

Financial Goals

Goal 1:

Goal 2:

Goal 3:

Where are you now vs. the desired outcome?

How will you feel when you have it?

How will you know when you have it?

What will this outcome accomplish for you?

Who else is involved or impacted by this goal?

Where, when, and how will you accomplish this?

What do you need to get your outcome?

Have you ever had or done this before? How did you do it?

Do you know anyone who has?

Can you act as if you have it?

Why do you want it?

Thoughts:

Physical Goals

Goal 1:

Goal 2:

Goal 3:

Where are you now vs. the desired outcome?

How will you feel when you have it?

How will you know when you have it?

What will this outcome accomplish for you?

Who else is involved or impacted by this goal?

Where, when, and how will you accomplish this?

What do you need to get your outcome?

Have you ever had or done this before? How did you do it?

Do you know anyone who has?

Can you act as if you have it?

Why do you want it?

Thoughts:

Educational Goals

Goal 1:

Goal 2:

Goal 3:

Where are you now vs. the desired outcome?

How will you feel when you have it?

How will you know when you have it?

What will this outcome accomplish for you?

Who else is involved or impacted by this goal?

Where, when, and how will you accomplish this?

What do you need to get your outcome?

Have you ever had or done this before? How did you do it?

Do you know anyone who has?

Can you act as if you have it?

Why do you want it?

Thoughts:

Personal/Mental/Spiritual Goals

Goal 1:

Goal 2:

Goal 3:

Where are you now vs. the desired outcome?

How will you feel when you have it?

How will you know when you have it?

What will this outcome accomplish for you?

Who else is involved or impacted by this goal?

Where, when, and how will you accomplish this?

What do you need to get your outcome?

Have you ever had or done this before? How did you do it?

Do you know anyone who has?

Can you act as if you have it?

Why do you want it?

Thoughts:

MY _____ GOALS

A goal is a **dream** with an **action plan**. Goals must be measurable, specific, time dependent, and written down.

Personal/Mental/ Spiritual Goals	Why is this important?	These are the steps required to accomplish my goals.	Date to accomplish by

Family Goals	Why is this important?	These are the steps required to accomplish my goals.	Date to accomplish by

Educational Goals	Why is this important?	These are the steps required to accomplish my goals.	Date to accomplish by

Physical Goals	Why is this important?	These are the steps required to accomplish my goals.	Date to accomplish by

Financial Goals	Why is this important?	These are the steps required to accomplish my goals.	Date to accomplish by

Three things that I know could get in the way of me accomplishing my goals:

1.

2.

3.

This is what I will implement to be sure that those three things never get in my way:

1.

2.

3.

I will give a copy of my plan to these three people and ask them to hold me accountable:

1.

2.

3.

When I accomplish my goals, this is how I will feel:

My Financials: Knowing My Numbers

Part One

Know how much it takes for you to accomplish all of your goals. The most successful people and businesses in the world are experts at "knowing the numbers!"

Secret: Most agents (and people in general) earn only what it takes to pay for their basic needs. This is why agents get into trouble at tax time – they did not budget for it. It's also why real estate agents often feel they are living from paycheck to paycheck. Use this formula to know what you REALLY need to earn to achieve your personal, business, family, and financial goals this year!

Monthly

A. Personal Overhead $_____

B. Business Overhead $_____

C. "Fun": This is the money necessary for you to accomplish all of your "fun" goals this year. If you skip this category, you won't have any fun! If it's not planned for, it doesn't happen. $_____

D. Taxes: Add up A, B, and C, and add 25% as a general rule of thumb. Some people pay more, some less, but 25% will allow you to prepare for taxes. $_____

E. Savings: All real estate agents say, "I want to save more," decide how much more. A good place to start is at least 90 days of personal and business savings. If you already have that, work on having one year of reserves saved. $_____

Add up A + B + C + D + E =
Income required to earn per MONTH =

$_____

My Outside Income is: $_____
(This is any non-real estate income, including spouse's income,
investment income, etc.)

The difference is: (Take **Income Required** from above, and
subtract **Outside Income**.) = $_____

It's okay if you don't have any outside income. Many agents
don't. But if you do have money coming in from somewhere
else, if it's predictable income, you need to account for it.

What I MUST EARN: $_____ / Month.

Take the amount from **What I MUST EARN**, and multiply it
by twelve to equal your required YEARLY income for personal,
business, savings, taxes, and fun. That amount is:
$_____. You will need this figure later,
when you use the Income and Unit Calculator, which shows you
how you're going to accomplish this income.

Part Two

The amount of my average net commission is:
$_____

Secret: If you're not sure, ask your broker if he or she tracked
this for you. If you're a NEW agent, find out the average sale
price in your area and use the average net commission based on
that price.

Secret: Net commission is what you KEEP after all broker
splits, any processing fees, etc.

Take the amount you must earn **per MONTH** and divide by
your average net commission. This will reveal the number of
transactions necessary to cover your personal, business, savings,
fun, and tax requirements each month.

Amount needed per month, divided by my average net commission = _____ deals needed monthly, x 12 = deals necessary yearly.

Part Three

I am currently averaging _____ deals per month.
This **does/does not** cover my personal, business, savings, taxes, and fun. (Circle your answer.)
I **am/am not** satisfied with continuing to earn at this level. (Circle your answer.)

Secret: If you keep doing what you've been doing, you'll keep producing what you've been producing – or – you'll slide backward as other agents pass you by who have upgraded their skills, education, mindset, and goal setting. Don't let this happen to you!

Am I motivated by **Fear**?

Am I motivated by **Incentive**?

What is **driving** me?

We will examine these questions more in our Goal Setting modules.

After completing the exercise above, **you know how much you must earn monthly and how many deals that requires you to produce.** Don't worry if it's more or less than you thought. Keep working through this business plan so you will have the confidence and the know how required to create your Real Estate Treasure – the amount required to achieve your personal, business, savings, and fun objectives, and also to pay your taxes. Budgeting and planning what it takes **now** will help you ensure your success throughout the year. Review this worksheet every two weeks to assist you in following your schedule, and make any necessary changes as you go.

Personal Budget

	Priority	Monthly	Yearly	Actual
Income				
Salary				
Interest/dividends				
Misc.				
TOTAL INCOME				
Expenses				
Home				
Mortgage/rent				
Home telephone				
Cellular telephone				
Home repairs				
Home improvement				
Home security				
Garden supplies				
Home Totals				
Daily Living				
Groceries				
Child care				
Dry cleaning				
Dining out				
Housecleaning service				
Dog walker				
Daily Living Totals				
Transportation				
Gas/fuel				
Insurance				
Repairs				
Car wash/detailing service				
Parking				
Public Transportation				
Transportation Totals				

	Priority	Monthly	Yearly	Actual
Dues/ Subscriptions				
Magazines				
Newspapers				
Internet connection				
Public radio/television				
Religious organizations				
Charity				
Dues/subscription Totals				
Personal				
Clothing				
Gifts				
Salon/Barber				
Books				
Music (digital, CDs, etc.)				
Personal Totals				
Financial obligations				
Long term savings				
Retirement (401k, Roth)				
Credit card payments				
Income tax (additional)				
Other obligations				
Financial obligation Totals				
Miscellaneous Payments				
Other				
Other				
Misc. Payments Totals				
TOTAL EXPENSES				
Cash short/extra				

	Priority	Monthly	Yearly	Actual
Entertainment				
Cable TV				
Video/DVD rentals				
Movies/Plays				
Concerts/clubs				
Entertainment Totals				
Health				
Health Club dues				
Health Insurance				
Prescriptions				
Over the counter drugs				
Copays/out of pocket				
Veterinarian/pet meds				
Life Insurance				
Health Totals				
Vacations				
Plane fare				
Accommodations				
Food				
Souvenirs				
Pet boarding/sitter				
Rental car				
Vacation Totals				
Recreation				
Gym fees				
Sports equipment				
Team dues				
Toys/child gear				
Recreation Totals				

Accountability

Secret: For optimum success, identify three accountability partners. These will be people who have similar goals, mindsets, and strategies as you. They do not have to be real estate agents, but may be. You may also choose to form a Master Mind group with them. The point is to hold each other accountable in a positive and supportive environment. Choose wisely and if someone isn't working for you, replace that person with a new partner immediately.

For a high level of Accountability, choose to do the following:

a) Email a summary of the HREU Daily Message to Accountability Partners and to yourself.
b) Send your Daily Plan Form to Accountability Partners.
c) Be accountable to your Master Mind Group.
d) Check in twice a day. In the morning, state your goals. At the end of the day, state what you accomplished. Help each other stay focused!

Minimum Standards of Accountability are as follows:

a) Daily Contacts: _____ per day.

EXP/FSBO/PCs/COIs/SS/REO

b) _____ appointments per week.

c) _____ time spent on scripts per day.

d) _____ time spent role playing per day.

e) _____ time spent doing Relentless Lead Follow Up.

My Accountability Partners Are:

Name: _____

Phone Number: _____

We communicate by:

_____

Name: _____

Phone Number: _____

We communicate by:

_____

Name: _____

Phone Number: _____

We communicate by:

_____

IMPLEMENTATIONS NEEDED

I understand that I must take action to find the Treasure as a result of my Business Plan. This means I may need to learn new things and form new habits and systems. I am committed to implementing these items within the first 90 days of my Plan: (Circle two to three maximum.)

*Sign up for courses at HREU to increase my skills

*Implement lead generation daily

*Stop fearing and start listing Short Sales and REO listings

*Sign up for the 1800homehotline.com system

*Listen to the free Friday interviews that I've missed, at

www.HarrisRealEstateUniversity.com, under 'free stuff.'

*Hire a buyer's agent

*Create/polish/upgrade my Pre-Listing Package

*Replace a team member

*Learn how to do Loan Modifications: www.AgentLoanModSecrets.com

*Read the HREU blog daily at www.TimAndJulieHarris.com

*Upgrade my Listing Presentation

*Upgrade/start using a Buyer Presentation

*Mail and call my COI/PC list consistently

*Mail JL/JS cards

*Develop a FSBO campaign of cards & calls

*Develop an EXP campaign of cards & calls

*Not just collecting but USING scripts!

*Actually develop/follow a Lead Follow Up System

*Create and use a buyer questionnaire

*Create and use a listing pre-qualification questionnaire

*Hire an assistant

*Sign up for a free coaching call at **www.TimAndJulieHarris.com**

DAILY CONTACT TRACKING:

Date: ___/___/___

> **Affirmation**
> Real estate is a people business. In order to reach my personal, business, and financial goals, I will speak with the maximum number of people daily. My goal is to be of service by determining how I can best serve the needs of those with whom I speak. This will result in daily appointments, listings, and buyers, and constant lead generation. I enjoy doing this because I know I am helping people who need my assistance.

A contact is a conversation with a decision-making adult about real estate.

Available appointment times that I am filling right now
(Fill in these appointments today.)

Date: _____ Time: _____ Listing/Buyer Name(s): _____
Address: _____ Price: _____
Why are they buying/selling? (Motivation) _____

Date: _____ Time: _____ Listing/Buyer Name(s): _____
Address: _____ Price: _____
Why are they buying/selling? (Motivation) _____

Date: _____ Time: _____ Listing/Buyer Name(s): _____
Address: _____ Price: _____
Why are they buying/selling? (Motivation) _____

DAILY CONTACT TRACKING:

Date: ___/___/___

Number of People with whom I have Spoken:
(Circle as you go!)

1 2 3 4 5 6 7 8 9 10 11 12 13 14 15 16 17 18 19 20 21 22 23 24 25 26 27 28 29

30 31 32 33 34 35 36 37 38 39 40 41 42 43 44 45 46 47 48 49 50 51 52 53 54 55

Leads Generated Today

Remember, relentless lead follow up is part of your daily plan. Transcribe these notes over to your Vital Signs or Top Producer ASAP.

Prospect's Name(s): _____ Phone: _____

Buyer/Seller/Both?: _____ Address: _____

Motivation/Reason for Moving: _____

Next step (CMA/Set Appointment/help them to be qualified to buy/etc.):

_____

Prospect's Name(s): _____ Phone: _____

Buyer/Seller/Both?: _____ Address: _____

Motivation/Reason for Moving: _____

Next step (CMA/Set Appointment/help them to be qualified to buy/etc.):

_____

DAILY PLAN TO REACH MY GOALS:

Date: ___/___/___

The Six Powerful Spokes
That Make the Wheel of my Business Thrive:

1)

2)

3)

4)

5)

6) Relentless Lead Follow Up
(Regardless of my other spokes, I am committed to following up on ALL existing leads DAILY. Lead follow up is a mandatory spoke.)

Today's Affirmations

1)

2)

3)

Today's Basic Schedule is:

Today I am working from _____ until _____. I have appointments at: _____.

I will stop working at ____, prepare for tomorrow and go home. This leaves me ____ hours to generate new business, follow up on leads, and negotiate contracts. I will use this time to make money so I can reach all of my personal, business, and financial goals this year!

I practice relentless lead follow up every business day.

Today I will follow up with these leads before I do anything else. I know that email doesn't count, so I will call them personally, and at a minimum, leave a message. The point of my lead follow up is to set appointments.

1) _____

2) _____

3) _____

4) _____

5) _____

Vital Signs Report

In order to get from where I am to where I want to be, I must develop strategies, initiate activities, measure results, and track my vital signs.

YTD Closed Transactions	Current Pendings	Active Listings	Active Buyers

Closings this Week	Offers I am working on this week	L Appointments this week	B Appointments this week

Hot Leads
Rate 'A, B, or C.'
(Motivation, A=L/B in next 30 days, B=L/B in next 60, C=??)

Name	$ Range	Motivation	Source	Next Appt.

Creating Your Powerful Moneymaking Schedule

FACT: If you were to interview the top agents in the country, you'd discover that all of them are serious about time management. They ALL follow a schedule that is based on their goals. They ALL stick to dollar productive activities. You've also heard the saying, "act as if," meaning, if you wish to achieve something, act as if you have it already. So it only makes sense to "act as if" you are already achieving your goals and dreams. This means following a schedule. Resist this skill at your own peril.   Lack of time management is the #1 arch-nemesis, goal-shattering issue for struggling agents. Break away from the crowd that lives month-to-month and join the ranks of those who control their time; for controlling your time means controlling your income.

How much time do you actually have to build your business?

To determine the number of hours you actually have available for building your business, calculate the number of daily hours you spend:

Per Day:

Hours spent sleeping: _____
Hours spent with family & friends: _____
**Hours spent on fitness, grooming, and other personal time:
_____**
Hours spent driving: _____
Total hours: _____

24 Hours minus TOTAL _____ hours committed to personal time = hours available to use in your powerful, moneymaking schedule. This will keep your schedule realistic.

The Importance of a Schedule

Can you name a professional who doesn't operate based on a **schedule**? Are there any? Lawyers, doctors, accountants, pilots, appraisers, and veterinarians all follow a schedule.

So does that mean that if you don't follow a schedule, that the public perceives you as **unprofessional**?

Ever wondered why real estate clients abuse your time?

When you work based on a professional schedule, you keep professional hours. If you don't keep a schedule, you won't work normal hours; the public will not respect your time.

Are you a "Pop-Tart" agent? Pop-Tart agents just "pop up" on the whim of any call from any person. They have no control over their emotions or over their time. They are also the very agents who continually complain about not having any time. Following a schedule is the only answer! Don't be a "Pop-Tart" agent.

Yes, you will have to get up at a certain hour regularly. Yes, you will have to prospect, or generate business regularly. Yes, consistent and relentless lead follow up is not only necessary, but required to achieve your goals. If you are saying, "But wait! I got into real estate so I wouldn't have to follow a schedule..." then you need to reconsider your goals. Agents who follow schedules achieve their goals. Agents to don't, don't. It is just that simple.

The good news is, that when you begin to take control of your time and operate with intention rather than being that Pop-Tart agent, you will find that you have **more time**, not less. You will find that you have **less stress**, not more. You will even discover that you feel calmer, more in control, and that your bank account is growing, just like your goals call for. Taking control of your time means taking control of your goals and ultimately of your life.

Won't that feel amazing?

Sample Schedule

6:30   **Exercise** (Secret: Many of our best prospecting students are also very consistent with their exercise programs.)

7:00   Prepare for the day

7:30   Arrive at work (home office/office, etc.)

7:30   Connect with Role Play and Accountability Partners

8:00   Call all NEW EXPIREDS

9:00   10-minute break

9:10   Continue with Expireds

10:00   10-minute break

10:10   New For Sale By Owners

11:00   10-minute break

11:10   Past Clients, Centers of Influence

12:00   LUNCH! Don't skip it, you need the energy!

1:00   LEAD FOLLOW UP: EXP/FSBO/PC/COI/Buyers/Short Sale/REO/Asset Mgmt/real estate agents who have shown your listings, etc.

2:00   Pre-Qualify leads and go on: Appointments, buyers and sellers. If no appointments, continue to prospect and do lead follow up or NEGOTIATE offers. Prepare CMA's, etc.

3:00   Special projects: mailings, tweaking this and that, preparing flyers, etc., one hour only until you have the business you desire.

4:00   Education for one hour: review past coaching calls, practice scripts, etc.

5:00   Go on listing appointments or go home. You've spent most of your day making money!

Goal Calculator

For Example:

Listing and Sales Goals Formula			
	Listings		**Sales**
Annual Real Estate Income Goal	$235,000		$125,000
Percentage of Total Income	35%		65%
Annual Dollar Income	$82,250		$81,250
Average Sales Price	$22,000		$22,000
Average Commission Percentage	3%		3%
Dollar Commission per Unit	$6,600.00		$6,600.00
Commission Level	65%		65%
Agent Dollars per Unit	$4,290.00		$4,290.00
Annual Dollar Income	$82,250.00		$81,250.00
Divided by Agent Dollars per Unit	$4,290.00		$4,290.00
Yearly Objective if all Sold & Closed	19.17		19.94
Divided by % of Units that Sell	85%		95%
Annual Units Goal	22.56		19.94
Divided by 12 (months)	12		12
Monthly Goal	1.88		1.66
	Listing Goal		**Sales Goal**

Listing and Sales Goals Formula			
Fill in your own goals here – fill in the shaded boxes.			
	Listings		**Sales**
Annual Real Estate Income Goal			
Percentage of Total Income			
Annual Dollar Income			
Average Sales Price			
Average Commission Percentage			
Dollar Commission per Unit			
Commission Level			
Agent Dollars per Unit			
Annual Dollar Income			
Divided by Agent Dollars per Unit			
Yearly Objective if all Sold & Closed			
Divided by % of Units that Sell			
Annual Units Goal			
Divided by 12 (months)			
Monthly Goal			
	Listing Goal		**Sales Goal**

My Sphere of Influence

Whom do I know?

What are the names of the members of your family?

What are the names of your spouse's family?

What are the names of your "extended" family?

> (People you consider family)

What is the name of your best friend?

What is the name of your spouse's best friend?

What are the names of your very close friends?

What are the names of your spouse's very close friends?

What are the names of your children's friend's parents?

What are your children's teachers' names?

What are your children's coaches' names?

What are your children's school principals' names?

What are your children's dentist's names?

What are your children's doctor's names?

More people I know:

What is your children's optometrist's name?

Who cuts your children's hair?

Who sells you your children's clothes?

Who is your children's school bus driver?

Who is your children's Sunday school teacher?

Who cuts your hair?

Free Coaching Call? http://1on1coaching.com

Who does your dry cleaning?

Who does your pedicures, manicures, facials?

From whom do you purchase gasoline?

Who services your car(s)?

From whom do you buy tires?

Who sold you your current car(s)?

From whom have you purchased cars in the past?

Who cleans your car(s)?

Who is your mailman?

Even more people I know:

Whom do you know at your church?

Whom do you see at the convenience store you frequent?

Who is the cashier you usually go to at the grocery store?

Who is your pharmacist?

Who are your doctor(s)?

Who are your spouse's doctor(s)?

Who is your Pastor, Minister, Priest, Bishop, Rabbi?

Who owes you money?

What is the name of your favorite teller at the bank?

From whom do you borrow money at the bank?

Who is your stockbroker?

Who is your financial planner?

Who prepares your taxes?

Who does your accounting?

Who is your Veterinarian?

Who grooms your pets?

I'd better be putting all these people into my database and sending them a regular newsletter!

Who takes care of your pets when you're out of town?

From whom did you get your pets?

To whom have you given your pet's babies?

Who owns your favorite restaurant?

Who waits on you most frequently at your favorite restaurant?

What is the name of your favorite bartender?

Who do you routinely see at your favorite bar or nightclub?

Who do you know on a first name basis at your country club?

Who do you play golf with?

Who do you ski with?

Who do you talk to at your health club?

Who do you play racquetball with?

Who do you play tennis with?

With whom do you attend your children's sporting events?

With whom do you go to concerts?

I should be calling five of these great people per day and connecting with them, asking them who they can introduce me to that could use my real estate services! (Referrals!)

With whom do you go to the movies?

With whom do you go to plays, theaters, galleries or museums?

Where do you go to breakfast and whom do you talk to?

Who is your attorney?

Who would you call if you had an air conditioning problem?

Who is your pest control person?

Who would you call to fix your roof?

Who would you call if you had an electrical problem?

Who picks up your trash?

Who is your Federal Express person?

Who mows your lawn/shovels your snow?

Who did your landscaping?

Who built your house?

Who is your landlord?

What is the name of the insurance agent who insures your homes?

I sure know a LOT of people!

What is the name of the insurance agent who sold you your life insurance?

What is the name of the insurance agent who handles your health insurance?

What is the name of the insurance agent who handles your car insurance?

Who do you buy clothes from?

Who is your tailor/seamstress/dressmaker?

Who do you buy make-up and/or cosmetics from?

Who did you buy your computer from?

Who fixes your computer?

Who fixes your other small appliances?

Who is your travel agent?

Who is your printer?

Who did you receive Christmas cards from last year?

Who did you send Christmas cards to last year?

Who changes your oil?

From whom did you buy furniture?

**I really should make this list my #1 spoke this year.
I can't believe how many people I know!
I'm committed to communicating with the people on this list
<u>on a regular basis!</u>**

Who repairs or upholsters your furniture?

From whom do you buy arts and crafts?

From whom do you buy office supplies?

Who do you see at your office building?

From whom do you buy your liquor?

From whom do you buy meat?

From whom do you buy fresh seafood?

From whom do you buy hardware?

Who do you know in law enforcement?

Who do you know in politics?

Who have you done business with in the past?

Who do you know at service organizations meeting?

  (Optimists, Loins Club, Rotary, etc.)

Who do you know from fraternal organizations?

  (Elks, VFW, Mason, etc.)

Who do you know from social organizations you're a member of?

Every time I have a closing, I'll add both sides of the transaction **to my list & make sure I speak to them regularly. They'll love to hear from me!**

Who do you know from trade or industry group that to which you belong?

From whom do you buy carpet, drapes, and appliances?

Who are your old high school classmates who are still around?

(Get out your yearbook.)

Who are your former coaches that are still around?

Who are your former teachers that are still around?

Who are your former school principals that are still around?

Who are your former college fraternity/sorority brothers/sisters that are still around?

Who are your college buddies that are still around?

Who are your military friends that are still around?

Who is your florist?

From whom do you rent movies?

Who did you invite to your wedding?

Who are your neighbors?

From whom did you buy your boat?

From whom did you buy your motorcycle?

From whom did you buy your motor-home/camper?

Who is your jeweler?

Who repairs your jewelry?

Who is your photographer?

Where do you get your pictures developed?

From whom do you buy your electronics?

    (TV, Stereo, etc.)

Who do you know in your homeowner's association?

What are the names of your co-workers from a previous job?

What are the names of your previous neighbors?

Who do you know from your child's daycare center?

What are the names of your spouse's past neighbors?

What are the names of your parent's best friends?

What are the names of your spouse's co-workers?

From whom do you buy advertising?

Who are the suppliers and vendors who come into your work place?

I seriously have no excuses but to be receiving at least five referrals per month from my powerful list of people I know!

Who is currently trying to sell you something?

Who made your will/living trust?

Who baptized your children?

Who performed your marriage?

Who delivers your water?

From whom do you buy shoes?

Who maintains your safety and security systems?

Who are your bowling buddies?

From whom do you play cards?

Who handles your communications equipment?

(Pagers, cell phones, etc.)

Who would lend you $100.00 with a phone call?

Affirmation

I am 100% committed to keeping this list updated. I'll review these questions quarterly and add to my database to make sure it is always growing. I know that when I communicate regularly with my Sphere of Influence, I'll receive a minimum of 10% return. That means if I only had ONE name for each of the 145 questions here, that would translate to 14.5 deals this year. If I do a REALLY great job, I could receive fare more than 10% return.

Affirmation and Important Quotes from Napoleon Hill

I believe that I will have this money in my possession. My belief is so strong that I now can see the money before my eyes. I am holding it in my hands. I know it exists and it is awaiting transfer to me in return for my services rendered with full honesty and all possible skill and diligence. A plan exists which will transfer the sum of _____ to me by _____ and my receptive mind will see that plan and cause me to follow it.

A goal is a dream with a deadline.

Action is the real measure of intelligence.

All achievements, all earned riches, have their beginning in an idea.

All the breaks you need in life wait within your imagination; imagination is the workshop of your mind, capable of turning mind energy into accomplishment and wealth.

Any idea, plan, or purpose may be placed in the mind through repetition of thought.

Before success comes in any man's life, he's sure to meet with much temporary defeat, and perhaps some failures. When defeat overtakes a man, the easiest and the most logical thing to do is to quit. That's exactly what the majority of men do.

Big pay and little responsibility are circumstances seldom found together.

Cherish your visions and your dreams as they are
the children of your soul, the blueprints of your
ultimate achievements.

Create a definite plan for carrying out your desire
and begin at once, whether you ready or not, to put
this plan into action.

Desire is the starting point of all achievement, not a
hope, not a wish, but a keen pulsating desire which
transcends everything.

Don't wait. The time will never be just right.

Edison failed 10,000 times before he made the
electric light. Do not be discouraged
if you fail a few times.

Education comes from within; you get it by
struggle and effort and thought.

Effort only fully releases its reward after a person
refuses to quit.

Every adversity, every failure, every heartache
carries with it the seed on an equal
or greater benefit.

Every person who wins in any undertaking must be
willing to cut all sources of retreat. Only by doing
so can one be sure of maintaining that state of mind
known as a burning desire to win –
essential to success.

Everyone enjoys doing the kind of work
for which he is best suited.

Fears are nothing more than a state of mind.

First comes thought; then organization of that
thought, into ideas and plans; then transformation
of those plans into reality. The beginning, as you
will observe, is in your imagination.

Great achievement is usually born of great
sacrifice, and is never the result of selfishness.

Happiness is found in doing,
not merely possessing.

Hold a picture of yourself long and steadily enough
in your mind's eye and you will be drawn toward it.

Ideas are the beginning points of all fortunes.

If you cannot do great things,
do small things in a great way.

If you do not conquer self,
you will be conquered by self.

If you must speak ill of another, do not speak it,
write it in the sand near the water's edge.

It has always been my belief that a man should do
his best, regardless of how much he receives for his
services, or the number of people he may be
serving or the class of people served.

It is always your next move.

It is literally true that you can succeed best and
quickest by helping others to succeed.

It takes half your life before you discover life is a
do-it-yourself project.

Just as our eyes need light in order to see, our
minds need ideas in order to conceive.

Man, alone, has the power to transform his
thoughts into physical reality; man, alone, can
dream and make his dreams come true.

Money without brains is always dangerous.

More gold has been mined from the thoughts of
men than has been taken from the earth.

Most great people have attained their greatest
success just one step beyond their greatest failure.

Nature cannot be tricked or cheated.
She will give up to you the object of your
struggles only after you have paid her price.

No accurate thinker will judge another person
by that which the other person's
enemies say about him.

No man can succeed in a line of endeavor
which he does not like.

No man ever achieved worthwhile success who did
not, at one time or other, find himself with at least
one foot hanging well over the brink of failure.

No man is ever whipped
until he quits in his own mind.

One must marry one's feelings to one's beliefs and
ideas. That is probably the only way to achieve a
measure of harmony in one's life.

Opportunity often comes disguised in the form
of misfortune or temporary defeat.

Patience, persistence and perspiration make
an unbeatable combination for success.

Persistence is to the character of man
as carbon is to steel.

Procrastination is the bad habit of putting of until
the day after tomorrow what should have been
done the day before yesterday.

Reduce your plan to writing. The moment you
complete this, you will have definitely given
concrete form to the intangible desire.

Strength and growth come only through
continuous effort and struggle.

Success in its highest and noblest form calls for
peace of mind and enjoyment and happiness which
come only to the man who has found the work that
he likes best.

The battle is all over except the "shouting" when
one knows what is wanted and has made up his
mind to get it, whatever the price may be.

The best way to sell yourself to others is first
to sell the others to yourself. The ladder of success
is never crowded at the top.

The majority of men meet with failure because of
their lack of persistence in creating new plans to
take the place of those which fail.

The man who does more than he is paid for will
soon be paid for more than he does.

The most interesting thing about a postage stamp is
the persistence with which it sticks to its job.

The starting point of all achievement is desire.

The starting point of all achievement is desire.
Keep this constantly in mind. Weak desires bring
weak results, just as a small amount of fire
makes a small amount of heat.

The way to develop decisiveness
is to start right where you are,
with the very next question you face.

The world has the habit of making room
for the man whose actions show
that he knows where he is going.

There are no limitations to the mind
except those we acknowledge.

There is one quality which one must possess to
win, and that is definiteness of purpose, the
knowledge of what one wants,
and a burning desire to possess it.

Think and grow rich.

Think twice before you speak, because your words
and influence will plant the seed of either success
or failure in the mind of another.

Understand this law and you will then know,
beyond room for the slightest doubt, that you are
constantly punishing yourself for every wrong you
commit and rewarding yourself for every act of
constructive conduct in which you indulge.

Victory is always possible for the person
who refuses to stop fighting.

War grows out of the desire of the individual to
gain advantage at the expense of his fellow man.

We begin to see, therefore, the importance of
selecting our environment with the greatest of care,
because environment is the mental feeding ground
out of which the food that goes into
our minds is extracted.

When defeat comes, accept it as a signal that your
plans are not sound, rebuild those plans, and set
sail once more toward your coveted goal.

When your desires are strong enough you will
appear to possess superhuman powers to achieve.

Wise men, when in doubt whether to speak or to
keep quiet, give themselves the benefit of the doubt
and remain silent.

You can start right where you stand and apply the
habit of going the extra mile by rendering more
service and better service than you are now being
paid for.

You give before you get.

You might well remember that nothing can bring
you success but yourself.

Your ability to use the principle of autosuggestion
will depend, very largely, upon your capacity to
concentrate upon a given desire until that desire
becomes a burning obsession.

Powerful Quotes

Secret: Everyone has tough days in real estate. The difference between agents who reach their personal, business, and financial goals and agents who live check to check is how they HANDLE the tough days.

Instructions: On difficult or stressful days, go directly to this page of powerful quotes. Read it from beginning to end, aloud, as many times as necessary until you are back into a powerful and productive mindset. You will feel a lot better and be able to get back to what is most important.

What lies behind us, and what lies before us are small matters compared to what lies within us.
Ralph Waldo Emerson

All life is a chance. So take it! The person who goes furthest is the one who is willing to do and dare.
Dale Carnegie

When you know what you want, and want it bad enough, you will find a way to get it.
Jim Rohn

The man who does more than he is paid for will soon be paid for more than he does.
Napoleon Hill

Success is doing ordinary things extraordinarily well.
Jim Rohn

Many of life's failures are people who did not realize how close they were to success when they gave up.
Thomas Edison

Edison failed 10,000 times before he made the electric light. Do not be discouraged if you fail a few times.
Napoleon Hill

It's time to start living the life you've imagined.
Henry James

Success doesn't come to you, you go to it.
Marva Collins

You have to believe in yourself when no one else does. That's what makes you a winner.
Venus Williams

We make a living by what we get. We make a life by what we give.
Winston Churchill

If you go to work on your goals, your goals will go to work on you. If you go to work on your plan, you plan will go to work on you. Whatever good things we build end up building us.
Jim Rohn

Take the first step on faith. You don't have to see the whole staircase. Just take the first step.
Martin Luther King Jr.
To guarantee success, act as if it were impossible to fail.
Dorothea Brande

Do not let what you cannot do interfere with what you can do.
John Wooden

Adversity is another way to measure the greatness of individuals. I never had a crisis that didn't make me stronger.
Elbert Hubbard

Don't wait until everything is just right. It will never be perfect. There will always be challenges, obstacles and less than perfect conditions. So what. Get started now. With each step you take, you will grow stronger, and more skilled, more and more self-confident and more and more successful.
Mark Victor Hansen

You have to learn the rules of the game. And they you have to play better than everyone else.
Albert Einstein

Success comes in cans; failure in can'ts.
Anonymous

Success means doing the best we can with what we have. Success is the doing, not the getting; in the trying, not the triumph. Success is a personal standard, reaching for the highest that is in us, becoming all that we can be.
Zig Ziglar

Most folks are about as happy as they make up their minds to be.
Abraham Lincoln

Your ATTITUDE is Everything

Secret: It is estimated that as much a 90% of success in any sales related field can be attributed to attitude. Have you ever noticed that the difference between YOU making a purchase and NOT making a purchase can be the attitude of the salesperson in front of you? In fact, it is not unusual for attitude to be the only difference between the person who is successful and the person who is not. Your expectations can lead to success!

For example:
When a listing opportunity arises, ask yourself if you are going out expecting success or failure. Are you going out to "make a presentation," to "meet with some sellers" expecting that the seller will cause you problems, or are you going out to **"take a new listing,"** expecting the seller to like what you have to offer, appreciate your expertise, and sign the paperwork? Expect failure and that fact will be evident in how you look, what you say, your choice of words, and your tone of voice. Expect success and you will prepare more carefully, take more support material and statistics with you, appear confident, and be relaxed. Remember that the bottom line is very simple. It takes no longer to "make a presentation" than it does to "take a new listing."

When working with buyers, do you take them out to "show some houses" or do you take them out to "find them their new home?" Many salespeople prevent themselves from making a sale the first day they are out with a buyer simply because they're convinced the person won't buy that day. Says who? Find them the right house and there will be no reason for them to put off purchasing it. Again, it takes no longer to "show property" than it does to sell property. Use scripts, presentations, and the right attitude to achieve all of your goals. You'll need to help a lot of people to help yourself. Stay focused and thrive!

Goal Worksheets

In this section you will find three sample worksheets. Ideally, this format is not just on these pages, it is posted on white boards on your office walls. Every top producer we have ever known or coached has posted three white boards on their wall. When we sold 100 homes per year our very first year and every year after that, we did the same thing. The power of visualization is magic. It works as added accountability, tracking, and motivation. In fact, one of our good friends, the top selling agent in Cincinnati, wanted to move from 100 homes per year to 200 homes per year. One of the things that cause this to happen for him was changing his "closed transactions" board from 100 to 150, and then to 200. Changing the board alone didn't accomplish his goals; it was the fact that he saw the board every day, that he filled it in every day. By having more slots to fill in, it caused him to take more action, different action. He had to change his lead generation, improve his lead follow up, and make several other changes. Without the visualization, he would have kept doing what he was doing, and he would have kept getting the same results. To change your results, surround yourself with your goals.

In addition to the white boards, one of your other walls needs to have your specific goals posted Use the chart we have included in the goal setting section. Again, surrounding yourself with what is important will improve your odds of taking the actions necessary to reach and even exceed those goals.

Do not skip this step. Do not say, "I don't want anyone to see that." The more people you share with, the more inspirational you will be to them. The more people you can inspire, the more inspired you will be personally. It is all connected, and we have 100% confidence that when you follow the Treasure Map, you will be amazed by your results!

Track Your Active Listings Worksheet

Seller Name(s)	
Listing Address	
List Date	
Expiration Date	
Source	
Last Spoke to on	
Seller's Motivation	
Original List Price	
Current Price	
Sell Me Now Price	
Commission to	
What to do TODAY to sell this listing	

Leads Worksheet: Example

Prospect Name	Buyer/ Seller	Motivation	Time Frame	Source	Date of Last Contact	Next Appt.	Pre-approved?
Bob & Jody Smith	Seller	Already moved to WI	Must sell ASAP	Expired	1/5/13	1/12/13	Already purchased
Christine Jones	Buyer	1st time buyer	Lease ends 3/1	Referral	1/6/13	2/1/13	FHA, in process
Louie Harris	Both	Downsizing	Not Specific	Farm	1/3/13	1/10/13	In process

Leads Worksheet

Prospect Name	Buyer/ Seller	Motivation	Time Frame	Source	Date of Last Contact	Next Appt.	Pre-approved?

Closed Transactions Worksheet

Address	Source	Sold Price	Commission %	Net $ to me	If listing, days on Market?
123 Example Street	Center of Influence	$500,000	3%	$11,500	127

Sent Thank You Card	New Address in Database?	Adopted other side in Database?	Asked for Referrals?	Asked for Testimonial?	Sent JL or JS card?
Yes, 1/3/13	Yes, entered	Yes, entered	Received	Yes, received	Scheduled for 1/15/13

What If I Need Help Completing My Treasure Map?

Follow this checklist:

➢ Have you read and completed all parts of your Treasure Map? If not, go back to the beginning and fill in any gaps.

➢ Are you missing any numbers necessary to fill in the math sections? Can you get those numbers from your broker? Most brokers track your income, average sales price and average commission percentages.

➢ If you still need help, visit our blog - www.TimAndJulieHarris.com. On the blog you'll find a button called **free coaching call**. Sign up for a free coaching call and our offices will schedule a call to assist you in the completion of your Treasure Map.

➢ If you are already enrolled in a regular course at HREU, such as Short Sale Secrets, REO Secrets, Scripts, Prospecting, Agent Tech, Buyer Agent Boot Camp, etc., make sure you are attending your regularly scheduled courses. Everything you learn there is designed to move you forward.

➢ If you need to enhance your skills, consider signing up for additional training with us at:

www.HarrisRealEstateUniversity.com

Made in the USA
Columbia, SC
27 November 2019